Getting Them Sober, Volume One
Action Guide

Also by Toby Rice Drews:

Getting Them Sober, Volume 1
Get Rid of Anxiety and Stress
Getting Them Sober, Volume 2

Getting Them Sober, Volume 1 Action Guide

by Toby Rice Drews
author of *Getting Them Sober, Volume 1*

Bridge Publishing, Inc.
Publishers of:
LOGOS • HAVEN • OPEN SCROLL

GETTING THEM SOBER ——

Getting Them Sober, Volume 1, Action Guide
Copyright © 1983 by Bridge Publishing Inc.,
All rights reserved.
Printed and bound in Great Britain by
Forsyth Middleton & Co. Ltd.
Library of Congress catalog card number:
International Standard Book Number: 0-88270-559-8
Bridge Publishing Inc., South Plainfield, New Jersey 07080
Valley Books, Gwent, U.K.

Contents

Chapter 1

No More Taking the Blame
for His Drinking!

Write About:

1. If you have not sought out help in Al-Anon, thus far, is it because of any of the following reasons?

    a. I am biased against it before I have investigated it.

    b. I think *my* situation is unique.

    c. I think the support group I'm in should be enough.

    d. I know I won't identify with those people.

    e. My sense of pride keeps me from going.

    f. I'm not a joiner.

2. What other reasons may prevent you from going to Al-Anon?

Suggested Activity:

Attend Al-Anon—at least six meetings. Try different groups (they won't all be alike) and tell yourself that you will identify, not compare yourself, with those attending.

Results:

What new activity (or behavior) have you been able to do, and what changes have resulted in your life?

Results Six Months Later in Me:

Chapter 2
Be Gentle With Yourself

Write About:
1. Describe a typical scenario, in your home, where you wind up feeling depressed and/or fearful and/or furious. (Perhaps you could write about the most recent episode of this kind.)

Suggested Activity:
1. Tell yourself, when you feel guilty for getting angry at the alcoholic—or when you tell yourself that you are overreacting —*that that is your disease talking.* Your disease tells you to minimize or deny what is really going on and take the blame upon yourself.
2. After attending at least one Al-Anon meeting a week for six weeks, look at the scenario you described (above), and see if your reactions to the alcoholic have changed. How have they changed?

Results:

What new activity (or behavior) have you been able to do, and what changes have resulted in your life?

Results Six Months Later in Me:

Chapter 3

Don't Worry About Whether He's Really an Alcoholic

Fact:

One of the early-stage medical symptoms of alcoholism is a change in the individual's tolerance for alcohol. This statement should not be confused simply with a high tolerance for alcohol.

A change in tolerance *usually* means: An alcoholic needs more *or* less than he did when he first started drinking, to get the same effect.

To give an example: Ned first drank at age fifteen. It took two beers to get a "glow on." Now, eight years later, Ned needs four beers to get that same "glow."

Ned's body has become addicted to alcohol.

In a later stage of alcoholism, the tolerance often *decreases*. In other words, Ned will, at some time (the body chemistries of alcoholics differ), need *less* alcohol to get that effect. His body is in a later stage of alcoholism and is reacting in a more toxic way to alcohol.

In yet later stages of alcoholism, Ned's tolerance will "flip-flop" all over the place. One day he can drink a gallon and not be able to get drunk; on another day, two beers may get him zonked.

Write About:
Has the tolerance for alcohol of the alcoholic in your life changed? Be specific.

Suggested Activity:
Whenever the alcoholic, or you, denies that he's an alcoholic, reread what you've just read and written.

Results:
What new activity (or behavior) have you been able to do, and what changes have resulted in your life?

Results Six Months Later in Me:

Chapter 4
Don't Pour Out the Booze

Write About:
If you try to stop him from drinking because you are afraid he'll die, or if you fear that if he dies, you will feel guilty because you did not prevent him from drinking, remember:
1. The idea that temporarily "saving" him, today, just *postpones* his final surrender to recovery.
2. You *cannot* watch him *all* the time.
3. If you *try* to watch him all the time, you will go crazy, and *still* not succeed in saving him.

Suggested Activity:
"Then, what can I *do?*" Go to Al-Anon and get yourself well. Then, there's a good chance that he will get well, too.

Results:
What new activity (or behavior) have you been able to do, and what changes have resulted in your life?

Results Six Months Later in Me:

Chapter 5
Learn to Relax

Write About:
If you tell yourself you don't have time to do fun/relaxing activities—fill this out:

MY TYPICAL DAYTIME CHART

TIME	TYPICAL ACTIVITY	TIME	TYPICAL ACTIVITY
7:00 AM		7:00 PM	
7:30 AM		7:30 PM	
8:00 AM		8:00 PM	
8:30 AM		8:30 PM	
9:00 AM		9:00 PM	
9:30 AM		9:30 PM	
10:00 AM		10:00 PM	
10:30 AM		10:30 PM	
11:00 AM		11:00 PM	
11:30 AM		11:30 PM	
Noon		Midnight	
12:30 PM		12:30 AM	
1:00 PM		1:00 AM	
1:30 PM		1:30 AM	
2:00 PM		2:00 AM	
2:30 PM		2:30 AM	
3:00 PM		3:00 AM	
3:30 PM		3:30 AM	
4:00 PM		4:00 AM	
4:30 PM		4:30 AM	
5:00 PM		5:00 AM	
5:30 PM		5:30 AM	
6:00 PM		6:00 AM	
6:30 PM		6:30 AM	

Suggested Activity:

1. Talk with someone about why you are not putting your health as a priority.

2. Schedule in at least two healthful activities per week, such as exercise.

Results:

What new activity (or behavior) have you been able to do, and what changes have resulted in your life?

Results Six Months Later in Me:

Chapter 6

Don't Be Afraid of Losing Him Because You're Changing

Write About:

1. Do you know you are not trapped?

2. Do you know that you *could* live alone even though you may not want to?

3. Do you know that everything is "upside down" in the alcoholic home? That is, the alcoholic is more dependent on you than he says or than you believe, and that you are *less* dependent on him than he says or than you believe, even though he's told you the opposite.

Write down your reactions to each of these thoughts:

1.

2.

3.

Suggested Activity:

Do one small action that may have terrified you before. It can be anything from bringing in pizza instead of cooking like the alcoholic may expect you to do, to going on a church trip that the alcoholic may have said you could not go on, threatening to "get drunk" if you do.

Results:

What new activity (or behavior) have you been able to do, and what changes have resulted in your life?

Results Six Months Later in Me:

Chapter 7
Stop Arguing With Him
(It Works!)

Write About:
If one builds up one's self-esteem and strengths in one area, there will be a ripple effect on all areas of one's life. Make a list of cultural and/or artistic and/or intellectual and/or physical and/or spiritual activities you'd like to do but that you may have been putting off. Work out a schedule to fit one in in the near future.

Suggested Activity:

When your alcoholic partner is "acting good" and you start to tell yourself how very wonderful he really is, remind yourself of the facts. Realize that you deny his very negative, unacceptable behaviors in this way.

Tell yourself at these times, when "all is good" that you will *not* be misled into feeling "terrific"; that you *will* be polite and kind and decent to him, but yet you will become more balanced in your perception of reality. You will even out more in your emotions.

Try out these new behaviors, one day at a time.

Results:

What new activity (or behavior) have you been able to do, and what changes have resulted in your life?

Results Six Months Later in Me:

Chapter 8

Do One Thing Every Day
Just for Yourself

Write About:

Does the suggestion that you should do at least one thing for yourself every day:

1. Make you feel guilty?
2. Make you feel anxious?
3. Make you feel slightly depressed?
4. Make you feel excited that this "prescription" is the way to get well?

Write about any of the above.

Suggested Activity:

For at least fifteen minutes today, do something that is pure fun.

Results:

What new activity (or behavior) have you been able to do, and what changes have resulted in your life?

Results Six Months Later in Me:

Chapter 9
Use Tough Love

Write About:
Does the thought of "tough love" make you:

1. Feel relieved?

2. Feel "down on yourself" for not helping a sick person?

3. Make you feel guilty that you do not feel guilty—just enraged at the alcoholic?

Write about any of the above.

Suggested Activity:
Do one *small* tough-love action this week.

Results:
What new activity (or behavior) have you been able to do, and what changes have resulted in your life?

Results Six Months Later in Me:

Chapter 10

Don't Ride With Him
When He's Drunk

Fact:
   If you are hesitant to insist that you should not ride with a drinking alcoholic who insists on driving, you are into a very dangerous form of denial.

Write About:
   List all the areas in which you change your behavior to accommodate the alcoholic.

Suggested Activity:
Tell yourself that just for today, you will try *not* to give in to life-threatening situations. Further, tell yourself, when you deny how dangerous a situation is, that even though you do not *feel,* yet, that it is dangerous, that you are probably into an insidious form of denial—and that that is your disease talking.

You don't have to *feel* something to go ahead and make a healthy change. Do it, and your mind will follow. When we stick to old, sick, self-demeaning behaviors, we "pay for it" in the long run. Some of us have chronic, serious illnesses; others get very depressed.

The pain of breaking away from someone else's illness is acute but short-lived, relative to the downhill roll of staying with it.

The payoff is healthful and life-enhancing.

Results:
What new activity (or behavior) have you been able to do, and what changes have resulted in your life?

Results Six Months Later in Me:

Chapter 11
Confront Him!

Write About:

If you are considering talking with the alcoholic about his disease, try to remember that all works out best if you leave the results up to your Higher Power. Write down all the positive things you can do *for yourself* after you talk with him. Make that list include places you can go for the afternoon or day or weekend, or longer, that would get your mind off the alcoholic situation.

Suggested Activity:

If you talk with him, pray for him (it's the *best* thing you can do) and remove yourself from the situation. Remember, God has His own timetable.

Results:

What new activity (or behavior) have you been able to do, and what changes have resulted in your life?

Results Six Months Later in Me:

Chapter 12
Walk Away From Abuse

Write About:
If you leave the situation, and stay away long enough to get past the immediate great-fear time, the fear will *diminish*. Write about your fears.

Suggested Activity:

If you can't leave now, instead of getting depressed, remind yourself:

1. The idea is "on the shelf."
2. You are not trapped.
3. For most people, leaving abuse is a *process,* not a one-time situation.

Results:

What new activity (or behavior) have you been able to do, and what changes have resulted in your life?

Results Six Months Later in Me:

Chapter 13
Accept Yourself

Write About:
Make a list of five small (or large) ways in which you can change your attitude and/or behavior, to enjoy your life more, for today—even if you cannot be in a different living situation today.

1.

2.

3.

4.

5.

Suggested Activity:
Do three of the above behaviors.

Results:
What new activity (or behavior) have you been able to do, and what changes have resulted in your life?

Results Six Months Later in Me:

Chapter 14
Don't Believe "Drunk Is Fun!"

Write About:

Make a list of creative ways that will enable you to get away from his disease.

1. For ten minutes or so:

2. For one to five hours:

3. For a day:

4. For a few days:

Suggested Activity:
Do one of the above today.

Results:
What new activity (or behavior) have you been able to do, and what changes have resulted in your life?

Results Six Months Later in Me:

Chapter 15

Tell Your Families? Only If *You* Want To!

Fact:

Most choices in an alcoholic household would be 100 percent easier to make *and* change, if necessary, if the drama were taken out of them.

Write About:

Write a paragraph about a choice you've made in the last few months that you thought was an important life decision that turned out to be unimportant.

Suggested Activity:
Think *today's* choices through. Ask yourself, when you get nervous about them, "What is the *worst* that can happen?"

Results:
What new activity (or behavior) have you been able to do, and what changes have resulted in your life?

Results Six Months Later in Me:

Chapter 16

Mean What You Say
and Say What You Mean

Write About:
Describe a recent event in which you did not act at your very best—where you did not act with confidence and good self-esteem.

Rewrite this scene, describing it in a way that shows you behaving as if you enjoy being you.

Suggested Activity:
1. Pretend you're on a stage, and act as if you enjoy being you when you are with others.
2. The next time the alcoholic looks at you contemptuously, tell yourself his disease is showing on his face. Then say a quick mental prayer for him.

Results:
What new activity (or behavior) have you been able to do, and what changes have resulted in your life?

Results Six Months Later in Me:

Chapter 17
Deal With His Arrogance!

Write About:
Remember back to a time when your alcoholic acted as if he didn't want you around, after something good had happened to him. Write it down. *Then,* remember what happened *afterward*—when he panicked, then needed and wanted your relationship again. Write down two or three incidents of this kind. Then remember, "This, too, shall pass," and refer to that when he's into arrogance again.

Suggested Activity:

The next time your alcoholic's co-worker or neighbor acts if the alcoholic is "terrific"—tell yourself:

1. That they only feel good toward him because he can charm them and make *them* feel *they* are attractive people.

2. They don't *really* care about him that much. They are only charmed because they know him superficially and when they are not around him, they don't think about him. So, it's just not all that important.

Results:

What new activity (or behavior) have you been able to do, and what changes have resulted in your life?

Results Six Months Later in Me:

Chapter 18
Don't Change Your Address!

Write About:

Keep a running list of your own denial—when you tell yourself, and perhaps tell the alcoholic, that the drinking is less of a problem than it is. (Example: Do you tell yourself that "you see 'it' too much?")

Suggested Activity:

Go to "open" meetings of AA (where non-alcoholics are permitted to attend) and listen for people's stories of how they had been into denial. Listen, and identify.

Results:

What new activity (or behavior) have you been able to do, and what changes have resulted in your life?

Results Six Months Later in Me:

Chapter 19
Hide the Car Keys?

Write About:
Write a paragraph describing the last time you accomplished one of your responsibilities, but did so with great drama and frazzled nerves. Incorporate any dialogue and thoughts that accompanied the situation.

Rewrite that scene, taking the drama out. (That includes using less emotionally laden words.)

Suggested Activity:

When you start to feel guilty that "you're saving yourself instead of the alcoholic, who is obviously dying"—tell yourself:

1. If *you* get calm, your children will have a good chance to get better, too, and therefore several people (plus *their* future families) will be able to avoid such a devastating illness.

2. Many Al-Anons and AA's have reported that *on the day she* let go, *he* got sober.

Results:

What new activity (or behavior) have you been able to do and what changes have resulted in your life?

Results Six Months Later in Me:

Chapter 20

You Have the Right To Get Sick Too!

Write About:

In order to dispel secret fears, it often helps to write them down, and it also often helps to ask yourself: "What's the worst that can happen?" Write your worst secret fears about getting physically ill and write how you *could* cope without the alcoholic.

Suggested Activity:

Accomplish one act today (mental and/or physical), that gives the alcoholic's disease back to him.

Results:

What new activity (or behavior) have you been able to do, and what changes have resulted in your life?

Results Six Months Later in Me:

Chapter 21
Learn About Blackouts

Write About:

Remember, and write about, an instance when you were fearful for the alcoholic, when *he* did not seem to be fearful, but glad *you* were fearful for him.

Suggested Activity:
One time, today, act as if you are not scared about a situation that had frightened you in the past.

Results:
What new activity (or behavior) have you been able to do, and what changes have resulted in your life?

Results Six Months Later in Me:

Chapter 22
Try To Remember It's a Disease

Write About:

Try to see that the alcoholic has a disease by looking at his condition in this way: He acts in roughly the same way as other alcoholics do; that is, his behavior is somewhat predictable. Realizing this, therefore, you can plan your actions better.

Make a list of some simple actions you can do to start changing your behavior around.

Suggested Activity:
 Try to put those behaviors into action.

Results:
 What new activity (or behavior) have you been able to do, and what changes have resulted in your life?

Results Six Months Later in Me:

Chapter 23
Let the Crises Happen

Write About:
Make a list of the alcoholic's other "rescuers," and write a paragraph next to each one's name, explaining, as best you can, why he or she probably *must*—for their own guilt or need to control—rescue your husband.

Refer to this list frequently. It will help to diminish your feeling of "them versus me." You will see them as *victims* of alcoholism, too—not powerful individuals, but people who need your prayers. Share your new-found knowledge about this disease with them.

Suggested Activity:

1. When the alcoholic asks you to rescue him, remind yourself that *he's* not asking; his *disease* is asking.

2. When you want to rescue, take a deep breath, pray, and remind yourself that this is difficult for *everyone*—the first few times. *It gets easier to say no to his disease.*

Results:

What new activity (or behavior) have you been able to do, and what changes have resulted in your life?

Results Six Months Later in Me:

Chapter 24

No More Lying To His Boss!

Write About:

Describe the last three instances in which you "helped" the alcoholic, and write down your feelings about how you thought he'd love you enough and feel grateful enough to get well—and how he didn't.

Suggested Activity:

The next time you want to rescue the alcoholic from his disease, tell yourself that this will not help him. Remind yourself that he is getting sicker, that his disease will not "hold still."

Results:

What new activity (or behavior) have you been able to do, and what changes have resulted in your life?

Results Six Months Later in Me:

Chapter 25

Start To Get Help—
Even Though He's the Drunk

Write About:

If you are the adult child of an alcoholic, make a list of persons whom you've dated and/or to whom you've been attracted. Write out how those relationships progressed. See if there are any patterns in these relationships.

Suggested Activity:

The next time you're very "high" on life (from a naturally "high" experience), remove yourself afterward. Take time to be alone. Calm your thoughts. This will help you to give yourself permission to not get as "low" when situations are not very pleasant.

Results:

What new activity (or behavior) have you been able to do, and what changes have resulted in your life?

Results Six Months Later in Me:

Chapter 26

Stay With Him—or Leave Him—
"Just for Today"

Write About:
You have a right to:
Stay with the alcoholic.
Leave.
Stay for today.
Leave—tomorrow.
Come back the next day.
Or any combination you choose.

And you are not crazy, no matter which you choose.

Write about what this means to you, for today.

Suggested Activity:

Spend one day telling yourself, *each* time you "get down on yourself," that you accept yourself as you are, that God accepts you and loves you as you are, and that is all that matters. This is a first step in getting well.

Results:

What new activity (or behavior) have you been able to do, and what changes have resulted in your life?

Results Six Months Later in Me:

Chapter 27
Break Out of Your Isolation

Write About:
1. The ways you have possibly isolated yourself.
2. What are your fears about ending this isolation?
3. What person can you contact to reestablish old ties?

Suggested Activity:

Reestablish a positive tie with an old friend—someone you have not talked with in a long time due to your isolation from being wrapped up in the alcoholic situation.

Results:

What new activity (or behavior) have you been able to do, and what changes have resulted in your life?

Results Six Months Later in Me:

Chapter 28

Stop Asking Permission!

Write About:

Write a paragraph on each of these incidents:

1. How you, over the past week, acted as if you were dependent on the alcoholic.

2. How you acted controlling of him, when all along you knew that you were reacting with fear, to stop him from hurting you. This was, in part, his unconscious way of pulling your strings to make sure you were "still there" to take care of him.

Suggested Activity:

Try not to react to his scaring you—and then *see* how *he* gets scared of that.

Results:

What new activity (or behavior) have you been able to do, and what changes have resulted in your life?

Results Six Months Later in Me:

Chapter 29
Act As If You Love *You*

Write About:

Write out a paragraph telling why:

1. You may feel that "acting your way to good feelings" won't work for you.

2. You may be afraid to feel better.

Suggested Activity:

Do *one* small action, today, that you previously believed you couldn't do until you were "emotionally ready."

Results:

What new activity (or behavior) have you been able to do, and what changes have resulted in your life?

Results Six Months Later in Me:

Chapter 30
Put Him in the Back of Your Mind

Write About:

Write out exactly how you feel about the *fact* that the alcoholic doesn't think about you as often as you think about him.

Suggested Activity:
Refer to what you just wrote whenever you become fearful, or worried about the alcoholic.

Results:
What new activity (or behavior) have you been able to do, and what changes have resulted in your life?

Results Six Months Later in Me:

Chapter 31
Don't Feel Guilty When You're Mad!

Write About:
Think the sick behavior through. Write down a typical scenario in your home where:

1. He does his "junk."

2. You act out your anger.

3. You get depressed because you feel guilty and trapped.

4. You feel despairing.

Suggested Activity:
1. The next time each scene happens, act healthily, with the faith that *each* step takes you towards renewed health that you've not known in years.

2. Keep telling yourself, *every* time you're afraid, that God will not punish you for your thoughts, that He is *infinitely* more loving and gentle and non-punishing than you could possibly understand or believe. Eventually, you *will* believe it.

Results:

What new activity (or behavior) have you been able to do, and what changes have resulted in your life?

Results Six Months Later in Me:

Chapter 32
Forget His Bad Mouth

Write About:
If you are involved with an alcoholic, and are also the grown child of an alcoholic, write about the times in your life when you've internalized others' criticisms of you, even when you *knew* they were trying to hurt you and that what they said *seemed* like it had substance, but was actually a gross exaggeration and/or distortion of fact.

Suggested Activity:

The next time a similar episode happens, act as if you are someone who can shrug off what is said about you. Talk it through with a wise person; consider the source; and go on with life, dismissing all negative thoughts.

Results:

What new activity (or behavior) have you been able to do, and what changes have resulted in your life?

Results Six Months Later in Me:

Chapter 33

Don't *Say* You're Changing—Just *Do* It!

Write About:
"The alcoholic hears what you do, not what you say; and the spouse hears what the alcoholic says and not what he does." Write about what this means to you—in practical terms, in actual incidences.

Suggested Activity:
For today, listen to what the alcoholic does, and not to what he says.

Results:
What new activity (or behavior) have you been able to do, and what changes have resulted in your life?

Results Six Months Later in Me:

Chapter 34

Stop Telling Him How To Get Sober (Don't Talk to Brick Walls Either)

Fact:

Alcoholism is a disease. Sure, the alcoholic may drink because the job/wife/weather "gets" to him, *but that's not what makes him an alcoholic.*

Some people react to stress by: eating; not eating; getting colds or flu; smoking; drinking, etc.

But if a person does not have a chemical predisposition to alcoholism, he or she will often not become an alcoholic just because she or he drinks. And conversely, if she or he has that chemical predisposition to alcoholism, it's fatal to drink at all. Many alcoholics are "instant" alcoholics: they became addicted to alcohol with their first drink—sometimes even as early as the age of five, six, or seven.

Some people have a more slowly progressing disease.

There is no test to determine whether or not you have that chemical predisposition or how early the disease's onset will occur.

Since alcoholism is truly a disease, the family is truly powerless to "make" someone become an alcoholic—any more than you can "make" someone become a diabetic. You might eat sugar to comfort you, but you won't become a diabetic, oftentimes, unless you are predisposed, chemically, to do so.

To Write About:
Put your feelings in writing about how this information relieves you of responsibility for causing, curing, or controlling the alcoholism.

Suggested Activity:

Some spouses feel guilty when they want to become less dependent on the alcoholic because they feel it's a betrayal, especially if they think, "I'll get strong and will then have the option to leave."

Another way to see this is to decide to become less dependent *merely* because it's healthy to do so. Wives who are married to healthy men are *usually* independent *because* that's a basis for a good marriage. Sooner or later, one of you will have to learn to live without the other.

Try to begin to take small, relatively stress-free steps to being less dependent instead of thinking, "Maybe I'll leave sometime in the future."

Results:

What new activity (or behavior) have you been able to do, and what changes have resulted in your life?

Results Six Months Later in Me:

Chapter 35

Don't Get Scared
When He Threatens To Drink

Write About:
List the areas in your life in which it would be easiest to make positive changes.

Write down three specific new behaviors you could develop in each of those areas.

Suggested Activity:
1. Start doing one of the above.
2. Bring up in conversation, in a sympathetic way, people whom the alcoholic has used in order to intimidate you. Do this frequently. Act as if you enjoy speaking of them instead of flinching at their names.

Results:
What new activity (or behavior) have you been able to do, and what changes have resulted in your life?

Results Six Months Later in Me:

Chapter 36

Wipe Out Saying,
"You've Been Drinking Again!"

Facts:
1. It doesn't work—it is not effective—to tell him "to stop."
2. *Not* reacting *will* work—getting at least *you* well.

Write About:
Write down all the physical and emotional problems you've experienced in your efforts to get him to stop hurting you.

Suggested Activity:
Remember that yelling doesn't work.

Remember that he's not "getting away" with anything when he's committed to drinking—he's dying.

Remember you'll experience guilt if you yell—and that *guilt* keeps you in the situation.

Results:
What new activity (or behavior) have you been able to do, and what changes have resulted in your life?

Results Six Months Later in Me:

Chapter 37
Don't Expect Him To Be Sober

Fact:
Faith is believing what you can't see at all.

Write About:
Think back in your life. Write about any situations where you wanted something very much, and you "forgot about it," and *then* it happened.

Suggested Activity:
Act as if you believe the reality of the alcoholic situation. This will free you and strengthen you in many ways.

Results:
What new activity (or behavior) have you been able to do, and what changes have resulted in your life?

Results Six Months Later in Me:

Chapter 38

Stop Checking the Bars

Write About:

Write a list of your assets. Write as if you were your best friend, telling someone else about you, expressing genuine excitement about your "new, terrific friend."

Suggested Activity:

In other areas of your life—other than dealing with the alcoholic—where it may be easier to begin to change, postpone instant gratification. Put off doing something unhealthy that you feel you must do. Success there will seep into more difficult areas.

Results:

What new activity (or behavior) have you been able to do, and what changes have resulted in your life?

Results Six Months Later in Me:

Chapter 39
Don't Beg Him To Stay

Write About:

If you are worried about losing an alcoholic, write out the times when he has threatened to leave and didn't, or the times when he left and then came back. Count them.

And, if he should leave because his disease drives him out, reread page twenty-nine of *Getting Them Sober* (Volume One).

Suggested Activity:

If you can't yet stop begging the alcoholic not to leave, tell yourself that:

1. It's just for today.

2. You're getting stronger—you're not weak, you're ill from living with alcoholism and you're recuperating.

3. You're putting the idea "on the shelf."

4. God will help you to do what is good for you.

Results:

What new activity (or behavior) have you been able to do, and what changes have resulted in your life?

Results Six Months Later in Me:

Chapter 40

Don't Be Scared That He Will Leave if He Gets Well

Write About:

1. Make two lists: what he's done for you and what you've done for the alcoholic. Seeing it in print often helps to crack through the illusion that you "don't do enough" and that he's the "strong and stable" one.

2. Write down the "payoffs" he probably gets when he "takes care of you."

3. Write down how your relationship has probably reversed itself—how he no longer takes care of you most of the time, but how you take care of him most of the time.

Suggested Activity:

1. Remind yourself that you have a right to expect your husband to care for you—emotionally and financially.

2. If the alcoholic tells you that, "When I get sober you'll be surprised at the number of women who will want me"—tell him that it's probably true. Smile. Then go back to what you were doing. If he stares at you, smile at him in an absent-minded way, as if you forgot what you were both just talking about. It will dissolve his "power" over you.

Results:

What new activity (or behavior) have you been able to do, and what changes have resulted in your life?

Results Six Months Later in Me:

Chapter 41
Getting Help

Write About:
Write about the times when the alcoholic has said or implied that you should change in some way. For instance, when he may have said that "legs look great with a tan"—and you panicked and spent hours sunning only to hear him say "It wasn't important."

Remember this list when you want to scramble to please him instead of taking care of yourself.

Suggested Activity:

Seek help in An-Anon. If you attend meetings and *try* to practice its program, you will get better despite yourself. That's a *promise.*

Results:

What new activity (or behavior) have you been able to do, and what changes have resulted in your life?

Results Six Months Later in Me: